Help the Environment

Reusing and Recycling

Charlotte Guillain

www.heinemann.co.uk/library
Visit our website to find out more information about Heinemann Library books.

To order:
☎ Phone 44 (0) 1865 888066
🖷 Send a fax to 44 (0) 1865 314091
📖 Visit the Heinemann Bookshop at www.heinemann.co.uk/library to browse our catalogue and order online.

First published in Great Britain by Heinemann Library,
Halley Court, Jordan Hill, Oxford OX2 8EJ, part of Harcourt
Education. Heinemann is a registered trademark of Harcourt
Education Ltd.

British Library Cataloguing in Publication Data
Guillain, Charlotte
Reusing and recycling. - (Help the environment) (Acorn)
1. Recycling (Waste, etc.) - Juvenile literature
minimization - Juvenile literature
I. Title
363.7282

1. Recycling (Waste, etc.) - Juvenile literature 2. Waste

Acknowledgements
The publishers would like to thank the following for
permission to reproduce photographs: ©Alamy pp. **11** (Kevin
Clifford Photography), **4 bottom left** (Kevin Foy), **10**
(ImageState, Pictor International), **14, 20 bottom left** (Mark
Boulton), **22** (Pat Behnke), **4 top right, 23 top** (Westend
61); ©ardea.com p. **13** (Mark Boulton); ©Brand X Pixtures
p. **4 bottom right** (Morey Milbradt); ©Corbis p. **19** (Susan
Steinkamp); ©Digital Vision p. **4 top left**; ©Getty Images
pp. **20 bottom right** (Blend Images), **18** (Photonica),
17 (Stockbyte); ©Pearson Education Ltd pp. **6, 7, 8, 9, 20
top left, 20 top right, 23 bottom** (Tudor Photography);
©Photoeditinc. p. **5** (Cindy Charles); ©Photolibrary pp.
21 (Index Stock Imagery), **15, 23 middle** (Stockbyte);
©Punchstock pp. **12** (pixland), **16** (pixtal)

Cover photograph of recycling bins reproduced with
permission of ©Superstock (age footstock). Back cover
photograph of children collecting cans for recycling
reproduced with permission of ©Corbis (Susan Steinkamp).

Every effort has been made to contact copyright holders of
any material reproduced in this book. Any omissions will
be rectified in subsequent printings if notice is given to the
publishers.

Contents

What is the environment?

The environment is the world all around us.

We need to care for the environment.

What is reusing?

Reusing is using old things again.

When we reuse things,
we make less rubbish.
We are helping the environment.

When we reuse boxes,
we are saving cardboard.
We are helping the environment.

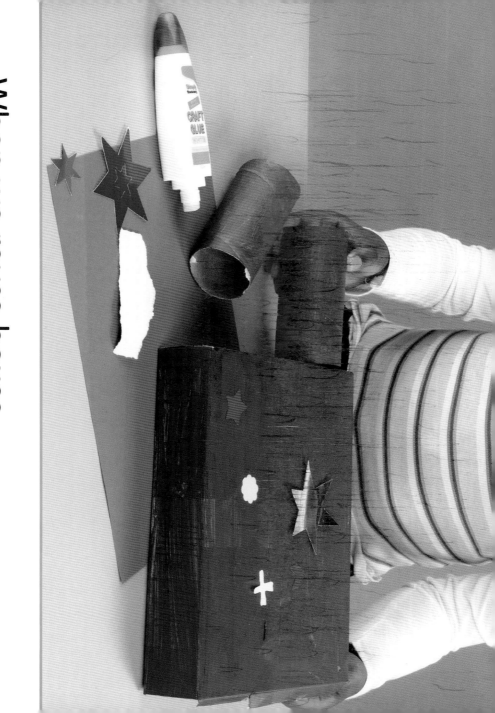

When we reuse paper,
we are saving paper.
We are helping the environment.

What is recycling?

glass bottles

Recycling is making new things from old things.

When we recycle things,

we are not wasting them.

We are helping the environment.

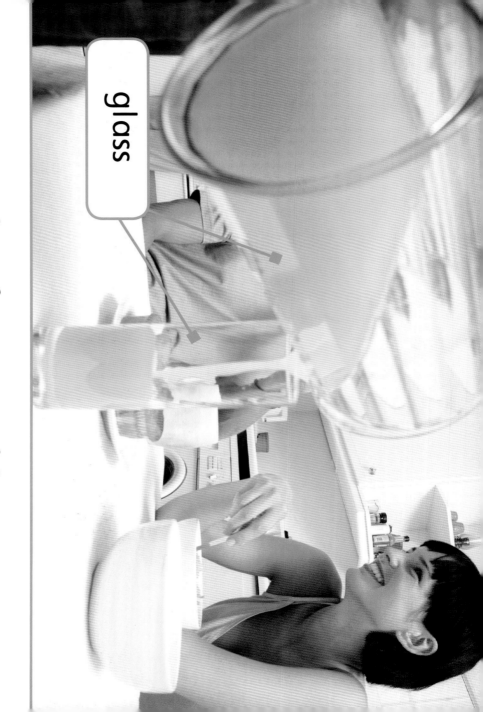

glass

We use glass for many things.

When we recycle glass,
we are not wasting glass.
We are helping the environment.

We use plastic for many things.

When we recycle plastic,

we are not wasting plastic.

We are helping the environment.

We use paper for many things.

When we recycle paper,
we are not wasting paper.
We are helping the environment.

We use metal for many things.

When we recycle metal,
we are not wasting metal.
We are helping the environment.

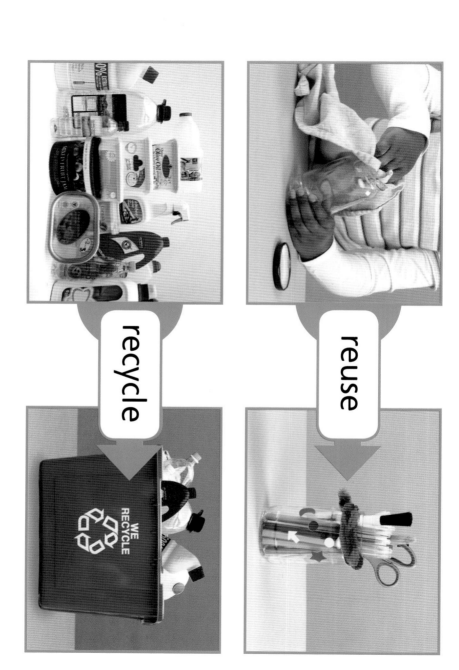

We can reuse and recycle every day.

recycle

reuse

We can help the environment.

How are they helping?

How are these people reusing things?

Answer on p. 24

Picture glossary

environment the world around us

recycle make old things into new things

reuse use again

Index

box 8

glass 10, 12, 13

metal 18, 19

new 10

old 6, 10, 23

paper 9, 16, 17

plastic 14, 15

rubbish 7

Answer to question on p.22: These people are buying old things so that they can use them again.

Note to Parents and Teachers

Before reading

Talk to children about reusing and recycling. Explain how it helps the environment. Show them a sock that is too small for them to wear. What suggestions can they come up with for reusing it? For example, using it as stuffing for a soft toy or making a sock puppet. Ask children to think about things that they can recycle, such as drink cans and paper.

After reading

• Make a 'catcher' from an old plastic milk bottle. Wash the bottle thoroughly. Cut off the bottom of the bottle and then cut a U shape under the handle. (NB Don't cut into the handle itself.) Decorate the catcher with coloured sticky tape. In the playground challenge pairs of children to see how many 'catches' they can do.

• Ask children to bring in any material that can be reused to make something new (used foil, egg boxes, newspaper, old wool, fabric, etc.). Draw a very large outline of an animal, such as a lion or a dinosaur. Help children cut up some of the material and decide where to place it on the outline to make a collage picture.

• Sing a recycling song to the tune of 'London Bridge is Falling Down'. For example, 'We recycle newspapers, newspapers, newspapers. We recycle newspapers to save our planet.' Sing other verses about plastic bottles, empty cans, and so on.